CAKES
ORDER BOOK

Enjoying this book?
Please leave a review because we would love to know your thoughts, feedback, and opinions to create better paper products for you!
Thank you so much for your support.

Business Information

Name:

Phone number:

Email:

Address:

City: State: Zip:

Company name:

Website:

Notes:

Order Index

No.	Order	No.	Order

Order Index

No.	Order	No.	Order

| Order no: | **Order Form** | Order date: |

Customer Details

Name: _____

Phone number: _____

Address: _____

_____

Delivery date: _____

Email: _____

Cake Details

Tiers: _____

Size & shapes: _____

Special instructions: _____

Cake :

Color scheme: _____

Flavours: _____

Notes

_____

_____

_____

_____

_____

Total cost: _____   Form of payment: _____

Order Form

Order no:

Order date:

Customer Details

Name: _____

Delivery date: _____

Phone number: _____

Email: _____

Address: _____

_____

Cake Details

Tiers: _____

Color scheme: _____

Size & shapes: _____

Flavours: _____

Special instructions: _____

Cake :

Notes

_____

_____

_____

_____

_____

Total cost:

Form of payment:

Order Form

Order no:

Order date:

Customer Details

Name: _____

Delivery date: _____

Phone number: _____

Email: _____

Address: _____

_____

Cake Details

Tiers: _____

Color scheme: _____

Size & shapes: _____

Flavours: _____

Special instructions: _____

Cake :

Notes

_____

_____

_____

_____

_____

Total cost:

Form of payment:

Order Form

Order no:

Order date:

Customer Details

Name: _____

Phone number: _____

Address: _____

_____

Delivery date: _____

Email: _____

Cake Details

Tiers: _____

Size & shapes: _____

Special instructions: _____

Cake :

Color scheme: _____

Flavours: _____

Notes

_____

_____

_____

_____

_____

Total cost:

Form of payment:

Order Form

Order no:

Order date:

Customer Details

Name: _____

Phone number: _____

Address: _____

_____

Delivery date: _____

Email: _____

Cake Details

Tiers: _____

Size & shapes: _____

Special instructions: _____

Cake :

Color scheme: _____

Flavours: _____

Notes

_____

_____

_____

_____

_____

Total cost:

Form of payment:

Order Form

Order no:

Order date:

Customer Details

Name: _____

Phone number: _____

Address: _____

_____

Delivery date: _____

Email: _____

Cake Details

Tiers: _____

Size & shapes: _____

Special instructions: _____

Cake :

Color scheme: _____

Flavours: _____

Notes

_____

_____

_____

_____

_____

Total cost:

Form of payment:

Order no:	**Order Form**	Order date:

Customer Details

Name:_____ Delivery date: _____

Phone number:_____ Email: _____

Address: _____

_____

Cake Details

Tiers:_____ Color scheme:_____

Size & shapes:_____ Flavours:_____

Special instructions: _____

Cake :

Notes

_____

_____

_____

_____

_____

_____

_____

Total cost:	Form of payment:

Order Form

Order no:

Order date:

Customer Details

Name:

Phone number:

Address:

Delivery date:

Email:

Cake Details

Tiers:

Size & shapes:

Special instructions:

Color scheme:

Flavours:

Cake :

Notes

Total cost:

Form of payment:

Order Form

Order no: _____

Order date: _____

Customer Details

Name: _____

Delivery date: _____

Phone number: _____

Email: _____

Address: _____

_____

Cake Details

Tiers: _____

Color scheme: _____

Size & shapes: _____

Flavours: _____

Special instructions: _____

Cake :

Notes

_____

_____

_____

_____

_____

Total cost:

Form of payment:

Order Form

Order no:

Order date:

Customer Details

Name: _____

Delivery date: _____

Phone number: _____

Email: _____

Address: _____

_____

Cake Details

Tiers: _____

Color scheme: _____

Size & shapes: _____

Flavours: _____

Special instructions: _____

Cake :

Notes

_____

_____

_____

_____

_____

Total cost:

Form of payment:

Order Form

Order no:

Order date:

Customer Details

Name:

Phone number:

Address:

Delivery date:

Email:

Cake Details

Tiers:

Size & shapes:

Special instructions:

Cake :

Color scheme:

Flavours:

Notes

Total cost:

Form of payment:

Order Form

Order no:

Order date:

Customer Details

Name: _____

Phone number: _____

Address: _____

_____

Delivery date: _____

Email: _____

Cake Details

Tiers: _____

Size & shapes: _____

Special instructions: _____

Cake :

Color scheme: _____

Flavours: _____

Notes

_____

_____

_____

_____

_____

Total cost:

Form of payment:

Order Form

Order no:

Order date:

Customer Details

Name: _____

Delivery date: _____

Phone number: _____

Email: _____

Address: _____

_____

_____

Cake Details

Tiers: _____

Color scheme: _____

Size & shapes: _____

Flavours: _____

Special instructions: _____

Cake :

Notes

_____

_____

_____

_____

_____

Total cost:

Form of payment:

Order Form

Order no:

Order date:

Customer Details

Name: _____

Phone number: _____

Address: _____

_____

Delivery date: _____

Email: _____

Cake Details

Tiers: _____

Size & shapes: _____

Special instructions: _____

Cake :

Color scheme: _____

Flavours: _____

Notes

_____

_____

_____

_____

Total cost:

Form of payment:

Order Form

Order no:

Order date:

Customer Details

Name: _____

Delivery date: _____

Phone number: _____

Email: _____

Address: _____

_____

Cake Details

Tiers: _____

Color scheme: _____

Size & shapes: _____

Flavours: _____

Special instructions: _____

Cake :

Notes

_____

_____

_____

_____

_____

_____

Total cost:

Form of payment:

Order Form

Order no: _____

Order date: _____

Customer Details

Name: _____

Delivery date: _____

Phone number: _____

Email: _____

Address: _____

_____

_____

Cake Details

Tiers: _____

Color scheme: _____

Size & shapes: _____

Flavours: _____

Special instructions: _____

Cake :

Notes

_____

_____

_____

_____

_____

Total cost:

Form of payment:

Order no:	**Order Form**	Order date:

Customer Details

Name: _____   Delivery date: _____

Phone number: _____   Email: _____

Address: _____

_____

Cake Details

Tiers: _____   Color scheme: _____

Size & shapes: _____   Flavours: _____

Special instructions: _____

Cake :

Notes

_____

_____

_____

_____

Total cost:	Form of payment:

Order Form

Order no:

Order date:

Customer Details

Name: _____

Phone number: _____

Address: _____

_____

Delivery date: _____

Email: _____

Cake Details

Tiers: _____

Size & shapes: _____

Special instructions: _____

Color scheme: _____

Flavours: _____

Cake :

Notes

_____

_____

_____

_____

_____

Total cost:

Form of payment:

Order Form

Order no:

Order date:

Customer Details

Name:

Phone number:

Address:

Delivery date:

Email:

Cake Details

Tiers:

Size & shapes:

Special instructions:

Cake :

Color scheme:

Flavours:

Notes

Total cost:

Form of payment:

| Order no: | **Order Form** | Order date: |

Customer Details

Name:_____   Delivery date: _____

Phone number:_____   Email: _____

Address: _____

_____

Cake Details

Tiers:_____   Color scheme:_____

Size & shapes:_____   Flavours:_____

Special instructions: _____

Cake :

Notes

_____

_____

_____

_____

_____

| Total cost: | Form of payment: |

| Order no: | **Order Form** | Order date: |

Customer Details

Name: _____ Delivery date: _____

Phone number: _____ Email: _____

Address: _____

_____

Cake Details

Tiers: _____ Color scheme: _____

Size & shapes: _____ Flavours: _____

Special instructions: _____

Cake :

Notes

_____

_____

_____

_____

_____

| Total cost: | Form of payment: |

Order Form

Order no:

Order date:

Customer Details

Name: _____

Phone number: _____

Address: _____

_____

Delivery date: _____

Email: _____

Cake Details

Tiers: _____

Size & shapes: _____

Special instructions: _____

Color scheme: _____

Flavours: _____

Cake :

Notes

_____

_____

_____

_____

_____

Total cost:

Form of payment:

| Order no: | **Order Form** | Order date: |

Customer Details

Name:_____   Delivery date: _____

Phone number:_____   Email: _____

Address: _____

_____

Cake Details

Tiers:_____   Color scheme:_____

Size & shapes:_____   Flavours:_____

Special instructions: _____

Cake :

Notes

_____

_____

_____

_____

_____

| Total cost: | Form of payment: |

| Order no: | **Order Form** | Order date: |

Customer Details

Name: _____   Delivery date: _____

Phone number: _____   Email: _____

Address: _____

_____

Cake Details

Tiers: _____   Color scheme: _____

Size & shapes: _____   Flavours: _____

Special instructions: _____

Cake :

Notes

_____

_____

_____

_____

_____

| Total cost: | Form of payment: |

| Order no: | **Order Form** | Order date: |

Customer Details

Name: _____
Phone number: _____
Address: _____
_____

Delivery date: _____
Email: _____

Cake Details

Tiers: _____
Size & shapes: _____
Special instructions: _____

Color scheme: _____
Flavours: _____

Cake :

Notes

_____
_____
_____
_____
_____

Total cost: Form of payment:

Order Form

Order no: _____

Order date: _____

Customer Details

Name: _____

Phone number: _____

Address: _____

_____

Delivery date: _____

Email: _____

Cake Details

Tiers: _____

Size & shapes: _____

Special instructions: _____

Cake :

Color scheme: _____

Flavours: _____

Notes

_____

_____

_____

_____

_____

Total cost:

Form of payment:

| Order no: | **Order Form** | Order date: |

Customer Details

Name: _____   Delivery date: _____

Phone number: _____   Email: _____

Address: _____

_____

Cake Details

Tiers: _____   Color scheme: _____

Size & shapes: _____   Flavours: _____

Special instructions: _____

Cake :

Notes

_____

_____

_____

_____

| Total cost: | Form of payment: |

Order Form

Order no: _____

Order date: _____

Customer Details

Name: _____

Phone number: _____

Address: _____

_____

Delivery date: _____

Email: _____

Cake Details

Tiers: _____

Size & shapes: _____

Special instructions: _____

Color scheme: _____

Flavours: _____

Cake :

Notes

_____

_____

_____

_____

Total cost:

Form of payment:

| Order no: | **Order Form** | Order date: |

Customer Details

Name: _____ Delivery date: _____

Phone number: _____ Email: _____

Address: _____

_____

Cake Details

Tiers: _____ Color scheme: _____

Size & shapes: _____ Flavours: _____

Special instructions: _____

Cake :

Notes

_____

_____

_____

_____

Total cost: _____ Form of payment:

| Order no: | **Order Form** | Order date: |

Customer Details

Name:_____   Delivery date:_____

Phone number:_____   Email:_____

Address:_____

_____

Cake Details

Tiers:_____   Color scheme:_____

Size & shapes:_____   Flavours:_____

Special instructions:_____

Cake :

Notes

_____

_____

_____

_____

Total cost: Form of payment:

Order Form

Order no:

Order date:

Customer Details

Name: _____

Phone number: _____

Address: _____

_____

_____

Delivery date: _____

Email: _____

Cake Details

Tiers: _____

Size & shapes: _____

Special instructions: _____

Color scheme: _____

Flavours: _____

Cake :

Notes

_____

_____

_____

_____

_____

Total cost:

Form of payment:

Order Form

Order no:

Order date:

Customer Details

Name: _____

Phone number: _____

Address: _____

_____

Delivery date: _____

Email: _____

Cake Details

Tiers: _____

Size & shapes: _____

Special instructions: _____

Color scheme: _____

Flavours: _____

Cake :

Notes

_____

_____

_____

_____

_____

Total cost:

Form of payment:

Order Form

Order no:

Order date:

Customer Details

Name: _____

Phone number: _____

Address: _____

_____

Delivery date: _____

Email: _____

Cake Details

Tiers: _____

Size & shapes: _____

Special instructions: _____

Cake :

Color scheme: _____

Flavours: _____

Notes

_____

_____

_____

_____

_____

Total cost:

Form of payment:

Order Form

Order no:

Order date:

Customer Details

Name: _____

Phone number: _____

Address: _____

_____

Delivery date: _____

Email: _____

Cake Details

Tiers: _____

Size & shapes: _____

Special instructions: _____

Color scheme: _____

Flavours: _____

Cake :

Notes

_____

_____

_____

_____

_____

Total cost:

Form of payment:

Order Form

Order no:

Order date:

Customer Details

Name: _____

Delivery date: _____

Phone number: _____

Email: _____

Address: _____

_____

Cake Details

Tiers: _____

Color scheme: _____

Size & shapes: _____

Flavours: _____

Special instructions: _____

Cake :

Notes

_____

_____

_____

_____

Total cost:

Form of payment:

Order Form

Order no:

Order date:

Customer Details

Name: _____

Delivery date: _____

Phone number: _____

Email: _____

Address: _____

_____

Cake Details

Tiers: _____

Color scheme: _____

Size & shapes: _____

Flavours: _____

Special instructions: _____

Cake :

Notes

_____

_____

_____

_____

Total cost:

Form of payment:

Order Form

Order no:

Order date:

Customer Details

Name: _____

Delivery date: _____

Phone number: _____

Email: _____

Address: _____

_____

Cake Details

Tiers: _____

Color scheme: _____

Size & shapes: _____

Flavours: _____

Special instructions: _____

Cake :

Notes

_____

_____

_____

_____

_____

Total cost:

Form of payment:

| Order no: | **Order Form** | Order date: |

Customer Details

Name: _____ Delivery date: _____

Phone number: _____ Email: _____

Address: _____

_____

Cake Details

Tiers: _____ Color scheme: _____

Size & shapes: _____ Flavours: _____

Special instructions: _____

Cake :

Notes

_____

_____

_____

_____

_____

Total cost: Form of payment:

Order Form

Order no:

Order date:

Customer Details

Name:

Phone number:

Address:

Delivery date:

Email:

Cake Details

Tiers:

Size & shapes:

Special instructions:

Cake :

Color scheme:

Flavours:

Notes

Total cost:

Form of payment:

Order Form

Order no:

Order date:

Customer Details

Name: _____

Delivery date: _____

Phone number: _____

Email: _____

Address: _____

_____

Cake Details

Tiers: _____

Color scheme: _____

Size & shapes: _____

Flavours: _____

Special instructions: _____

Cake :

Notes

_____

_____

_____

_____

_____

Total cost:

Form of payment:

Order Form

Order no:

Order date:

Customer Details

Name:

Phone number:

Address:

Delivery date:

Email:

Cake Details

Tiers:

Size & shapes:

Special instructions:

Cake :

Color scheme:

Flavours:

Notes

Total cost:

Form of payment:

| Order no: | **Order Form** | Order date: |

Customer Details

Name: _____ Delivery date: _____

Phone number: _____ Email: _____

Address: _____

_____

Cake Details

Tiers: _____ Color scheme: _____

Size & shapes: _____ Flavours: _____

Special instructions: _____

Cake :

Notes

_____

_____

_____

_____

Total cost: Form of payment:

| Order no: | **Order Form** | Order date: |

Customer Details

Name:_____ Delivery date:_____

Phone number:_____ Email:_____

Address:_____

_____

Cake Details

Tiers:_____ Color scheme:_____

Size & shapes:_____ Flavours:_____

Special instructions:_____

Cake :

Notes

_____

_____

_____

_____

_____

Total cost: Form of payment:

Order Form

Order no:		Order date:

Customer Details

Name: _____   Delivery date: _____

Phone number: _____   Email: _____

Address: _____

_____

Cake Details

Tiers: _____   Color scheme: _____

Size & shapes: _____   Flavours: _____

Special instructions: _____

Cake :

Notes

_____

_____

_____

_____

Total cost:	Form of payment:

| Order no: | **Order Form** | Order date: |

Customer Details

Name:_____   Delivery date:_____

Phone number:_____   Email:_____

Address:_____

_____

Cake Details

Tiers:_____   Color scheme:_____

Size & shapes:_____   Flavours:_____

Special instructions:_____

Cake :

Notes

_____

_____

_____

_____

_____

Total cost: Form of payment:

| Order no: | **Order Form** | Order date: |

Customer Details

Name: _____ Delivery date: _____

Phone number: _____ Email: _____

Address: _____

_____

Cake Details

Tiers: _____ Color scheme: _____

Size & shapes: _____ Flavours: _____

Special instructions: _____

Cake :

Notes

_____

_____

_____

_____

_____

| Total cost: | Form of payment: |

| Order no: | **Order Form** | Order date: |

Customer Details

Name: _____   Delivery date: _____

Phone number: _____   Email: _____

Address: _____

_____

Cake Details

Tiers: _____   Color scheme: _____

Size & shapes: _____   Flavours: _____

Special instructions: _____

Cake :

Notes

_____

_____

_____

_____

| Total cost: | Form of payment: |

Order Form

Order no:

Order date:

Customer Details

Name:

Phone number:

Address:

Delivery date:

Email:

Cake Details

Tiers:

Size & shapes:

Special instructions:

Cake :

Color scheme:

Flavours:

Notes

Total cost:

Form of payment:

Order Form

Order no:

Order date:

Customer Details

Name:

Phone number:

Address:

Delivery date:

Email:

Cake Details

Tiers:

Size & shapes:

Special instructions:

Cake :

Color scheme:

Flavours:

Notes

Total cost:

Form of payment:

Order no:	**Order Form**	Order date:

Customer Details

Name: _____ Delivery date: _____

Phone number: _____ Email: _____

Address: _____

_____

Cake Details

Tiers: _____ Color scheme: _____

Size & shapes: _____ Flavours: _____

Special instructions: _____

Cake :

Notes

_____

_____

_____

_____

_____

Total cost:	Form of payment:

Order no:	**Order Form**	Order date:

Customer Details

Name:_____

Phone number:_____

Address: _____
_____

Delivery date: _____

Email: _____

Cake Details

Tiers:_____

Size & shapes:_____

Special instructions: _____

Cake :

Color scheme:_____

Flavours:_____

Notes

_____
_____
_____
_____
_____

Total cost:

Form of payment:

Order Form

Order no:

Order date:

Customer Details

Name: _____

Delivery date: _____

Phone number: _____

Email: _____

Address: _____

_____

Cake Details

Tiers: _____

Color scheme: _____

Size & shapes: _____

Flavours: _____

Special instructions: _____

Cake :

Notes

_____

_____

_____

_____

_____

Total cost:

Form of payment:

Order Form

Order no:

Order date:

Customer Details

Name:_____

Delivery date:_____

Phone number:_____

Email:_____

Address:_____

_____

Cake Details

Tiers:_____

Color scheme:_____

Size & shapes:_____

Flavours:_____

Special instructions:_____

Cake :

Notes

_____

_____

_____

_____

_____

Total cost:

Form of payment:

Order Form

Order no:

Order date:

Customer Details

Name: _____

Phone number: _____

Address: _____

_____

Delivery date: _____

Email: _____

Cake Details

Tiers: _____

Size & shapes: _____

Special instructions: _____

Color scheme: _____

Flavours: _____

Cake :

Notes

_____

_____

_____

_____

Total cost:

Form of payment:

Order Form

Order no:

Order date:

Customer Details

Name:

Phone number:

Address:

Delivery date:

Email:

Cake Details

Tiers:

Size & shapes:

Special instructions:

Cake :

Color scheme:

Flavours:

Notes

Total cost:

Form of payment:

Order Form

| Order no: | **Order Form** | Order date: |

Customer Details

Name: _____

Phone number: _____

Address: _____

_____

Delivery date: _____

Email: _____

Cake Details

Tiers: _____

Size & shapes: _____

Special instructions: _____

Cake :

Color scheme: _____

Flavours: _____

Notes

_____

_____

_____

_____

Total cost: _____

Form of payment: _____

Order no: **Order Form**   **Order date:**

Customer Details

Name:_____   Delivery date:_____

Phone number:_____   Email:_____

Address: _____

_____

Cake Details

Tiers:_____   Color scheme:_____

Size & shapes:_____   Flavours:_____

Special instructions: _____

Cake :

Notes

_____

_____

_____

_____

_____

_____

Total cost: **Form of payment:**

Order Form

Order no:

Order date:

Customer Details

Name: _____

Delivery date: _____

Phone number: _____

Email: _____

Address: _____

_____

Cake Details

Tiers: _____

Color scheme: _____

Size & shapes: _____

Flavours: _____

Special instructions: _____

Cake :

Notes

_____

_____

_____

_____

Total cost:

Form of payment:

Order Form

Order no:

Order date:

Customer Details

Name:

Phone number:

Address:

Delivery date:

Email:

Cake Details

Tiers:

Size & shapes:

Special instructions:

Color scheme:

Flavours:

Cake :

Notes

Total cost:

Form of payment:

Order Form

Order no:

Order date:

Customer Details

Name: _____

Delivery date: _____

Phone number: _____

Email: _____

Address: _____

_____

Cake Details

Tiers: _____

Color scheme: _____

Size & shapes: _____

Flavours: _____

Special instructions: _____

Cake :

Notes

_____

_____

_____

_____

Total cost:

Form of payment:

| Order no: | **Order Form** | Order date: |

Customer Details

Name:_____ Delivery date:_____

Phone number:_____ Email:_____

Address:_____

_____

Cake Details

Tiers:_____ Color scheme:_____

Size & shapes:_____ Flavours:_____

Special instructions:_____

Cake :

Notes

_____

_____

_____

_____

_____

_____

Total cost: Form of payment:

Order Form

Order no:

Order date:

Customer Details

Name: _____

Phone number: _____

Address: _____

_____

Delivery date: _____

Email: _____

Cake Details

Tiers: _____

Size & shapes: _____

Special instructions: _____

Cake :

Color scheme: _____

Flavours: _____

Notes

_____

_____

_____

_____

_____

Total cost:

Form of payment:

Order Form

Order no:

Order date:

Customer Details

Name: _____

Phone number: _____

Address: _____

_____

Delivery date: _____

Email: _____

Cake Details

Tiers: _____

Size & shapes: _____

Special instructions: _____

Cake :

Color scheme: _____

Flavours: _____

Notes

_____

_____

_____

_____

_____

Total cost:

Form of payment:

Order Form

Order no:

Order date:

Customer Details

Name: _____

Phone number: _____

Address: _____

_____

Delivery date: _____

Email: _____

Cake Details

Tiers: _____

Size & shapes: _____

Special instructions: _____

Cake :

Color scheme: _____

Flavours: _____

Notes

_____

_____

_____

_____

Total cost:

Form of payment:

Order Form

Order no:

Order date:

Customer Details

Name: _____

Delivery date: _____

Phone number: _____

Email: _____

Address: _____

_____

Cake Details

Tiers: _____

Color scheme: _____

Size & shapes: _____

Flavours: _____

Special instructions: _____

Cake :

Notes

_____

_____

_____

_____

_____

Total cost:

Form of payment:

Order Form

Order no:

Order date:

Customer Details

Name:

Phone number:

Address:

Delivery date:

Email:

Cake Details

Tiers:

Size & shapes:

Special instructions:

Cake :

Color scheme:

Flavours:

Notes

Total cost:

Form of payment:

Order Form

Order no:

Order date:

Customer Details

Name: _____

Delivery date: _____

Phone number: _____

Email: _____

Address: _____

_____

Cake Details

Tiers: _____

Color scheme: _____

Size & shapes: _____

Flavours: _____

Special instructions: _____

Cake :

Notes

_____

_____

_____

_____

_____

Total cost:

Form of payment:

Order Form

Order no:

Order date:

Customer Details

Name: _____

Phone number: _____

Address: _____
_____

Delivery date: _____

Email: _____

Cake Details

Tiers: _____

Size & shapes: _____

Special instructions: _____

Cake :

Color scheme: _____

Flavours: _____

Notes

_____
_____
_____
_____
_____

Total cost:

Form of payment:

Customer Details

Name: _____   Delivery date: _____

Phone number: _____   Email: _____

Address: _____

_____

Cake Details

Tiers: _____ Color scheme: _____

Size & shapes: _____ Flavours: _____

Special instructions: _____

Cake :

Notes

_____

_____

_____

_____

_____

_____

Total cost: Form of payment:

| Order no: | **Order Form** | Order date: |

Customer Details

Name: _____ Delivery date: _____

Phone number: _____ Email: _____

Address: _____

_____

Cake Details

Tiers: _____ Color scheme: _____

Size & shapes: _____ Flavours: _____

Special instructions: _____

Cake :

Notes

_____

_____

_____

_____

_____

| Total cost: | Form of payment: |

Order Form

Order no:

Order date:

Customer Details

Name: _____

Phone number: _____

Address: _____

_____

Delivery date: _____

Email: _____

Cake Details

Tiers: _____

Size & shapes: _____

Special instructions: _____

Cake :

Color scheme: _____

Flavours: _____

Notes

_____

_____

_____

_____

_____

Total cost:

Form of payment:

Order Form

Order no:

Order date:

Customer Details

Name: _____

Phone number: _____

Address: _____

_____

Delivery date: _____

Email: _____

Cake Details

Tiers: _____

Size & shapes: _____

Special instructions: _____

Cake :

Color scheme: _____

Flavours: _____

Notes

_____

_____

_____

_____

Total cost:

Form of payment:

Order Form

Order no:

Order date:

Customer Details

Name: _____

Phone number: _____

Address: _____

_____

Delivery date: _____

Email: _____

Cake Details

Tiers: _____

Size & shapes: _____

Special instructions: _____

Color scheme: _____

Flavours: _____

Cake :

Notes

_____

_____

_____

_____

_____

Total cost:

Form of payment:

Order Form

Order no:

Order date:

Customer Details

Name: _____

Phone number: _____

Address: _____
_____
_____

Delivery date: _____

Email: _____

Cake Details

Tiers: _____

Size & shapes: _____

Special instructions: _____

Cake :

Color scheme: _____

Flavours: _____

Notes

_____
_____
_____
_____
_____

Total cost:

Form of payment:

Order Form

Order no:

Order date:

Customer Details

Name:

Phone number:

Address:

Delivery date:

Email:

Cake Details

Tiers:

Size & shapes:

Special instructions:

Color scheme:

Flavours:

Cake :

Notes

Total cost:

Form of payment:

Order Form

Order no:

Order date:

Customer Details

Name: _____

Phone number: _____

Address: _____

_____

Delivery date: _____

Email: _____

Cake Details

Tiers: _____

Size & shapes: _____

Special instructions: _____

Cake :

Color scheme: _____

Flavours: _____

Notes

_____

_____

_____

_____

_____

Total cost:

Form of payment:

| Order no: | Order Form | Order date: |

Customer Details

Name:_____ Delivery date: _____

Phone number:_____ Email: _____

Address: _____

_____

Cake Details

Tiers:_____ Color scheme:_____

Size & shapes:_____ Flavours:_____

Special instructions: _____

Cake :

Notes

_____

_____

_____

_____

| Total cost: | Form of payment: |

Order Form

Order no:

Order date:

Customer Details

Name: _____

Delivery date: _____

Phone number: _____

Email: _____

Address: _____

_____

Cake Details

Tiers: _____

Color scheme: _____

Size & shapes: _____

Flavours: _____

Special instructions: _____

Cake :

Notes

_____

_____

_____

_____

_____

_____

Total cost:

Form of payment:

Order Form

Order no:

Order date:

Customer Details

Name: _____

Phone number: _____

Address: _____

_____

Delivery date: _____

Email: _____

Cake Details

Tiers: _____

Size & shapes: _____

Special instructions: _____

Cake :

Color scheme: _____

Flavours: _____

Notes

_____

_____

_____

_____

_____

Total cost:

Form of payment:

| Order no: | **Order Form** | Order date: |

Customer Details

Name: _____ Delivery date: _____

Phone number: _____ Email: _____

Address: _____

_____

_____

Cake Details

Tiers: _____ Color scheme: _____

Size & shapes: _____ Flavours: _____

Special instructions: _____

Cake :

Notes

_____

_____

_____

_____

_____

| Total cost: | Form of payment: |

Order Form

Order no: _____

Order date: _____

Customer Details

Name: _____

Phone number: _____

Address: _____

_____

Delivery date: _____

Email: _____

Cake Details

Tiers: _____

Size & shapes: _____

Special instructions: _____

Cake :

Color scheme: _____

Flavours: _____

Notes

_____

_____

_____

_____

_____

Total cost:

Form of payment:

Order Form

Order no: Order date:

Customer Details

Name: _____   Delivery date: _____

Phone number: _____   Email: _____

Address: _____

_____

Cake Details

Tiers: _____   Color scheme: _____

Size & shapes: _____   Flavours: _____

Special instructions: _____

Cake :

Notes

_____

_____

_____

_____

_____

Total cost: Form of payment:

Order Form

Order no:

Order date:

Customer Details

Name: _____

Delivery date: _____

Phone number: _____

Email: _____

Address: _____

_____

Cake Details

Tiers: _____

Color scheme: _____

Size & shapes: _____

Flavours: _____

Special instructions: _____

Cake :

Notes

_____

_____

_____

_____

_____

Total cost:

Form of payment:

Order Form

Order no:

Order date:

Customer Details

Name: _____

Phone number: _____

Address: _____

_____

Delivery date: _____

Email: _____

Cake Details

Tiers: _____

Size & shapes: _____

Special instructions: _____

Color scheme: _____

Flavours: _____

Cake :

Notes

_____

_____

_____

_____

_____

Total cost:

Form of payment:

| Order no: | **Order Form** | Order date: |

Customer Details

Name: _____ Delivery date: _____

Phone number: _____ Email: _____

Address: _____

_____

Cake Details

Tiers: _____ Color scheme: _____

Size & shapes: _____ Flavours: _____

Special instructions: _____

Cake :

Notes

_____

_____

_____

_____

_____

| Total cost: | Form of payment: |

Order Form

Order no:

Order date:

Customer Details

Name: _____

Phone number: _____

Address: _____
_____

Delivery date: _____

Email: _____

Cake Details

Tiers: _____

Size & shapes: _____

Special instructions: _____

Cake :

Color scheme: _____

Flavours: _____

Notes

_____
_____
_____
_____

Total cost:

Form of payment:

Order Form

Order no:

Order date:

Customer Details

Name: _____

Delivery date: _____

Phone number: _____

Email: _____

Address: _____

_____

Cake Details

Tiers: _____

Color scheme: _____

Size & shapes: _____

Flavours: _____

Special instructions: _____

Cake :

Notes

_____

_____

_____

_____

_____

Total cost:

Form of payment:

| Order no: | **Order Form** | Order date: |

Customer Details

Name:_____   Delivery date: _____

Phone number:_____   Email: _____

Address: _____

_____

Cake Details

Tiers:_____   Color scheme:_____

Size & shapes:_____   Flavours:_____

Special instructions: _____

Cake :

Notes

_____

_____

_____

_____

_____

_____

| Total cost: | Form of payment: |

Order Form

Order no:

Order date:

Customer Details

Name: _____

Phone number: _____

Address: _____

_____

Delivery date: _____

Email: _____

Cake Details

Tiers: _____

Size & shapes: _____

Special instructions: _____

Cake :

Color scheme: _____

Flavours: _____

Notes

_____

_____

_____

_____

_____

Total cost:

Form of payment:

Order Form

Order no:

Order date:

Customer Details

Name: _____

Phone number: _____

Address: _____

_____

Delivery date: _____

Email: _____

Cake Details

Tiers: _____

Size & shapes: _____

Special instructions: _____

Cake :

Color scheme: _____

Flavours: _____

Notes

_____

_____

_____

_____

_____

Total cost:

Form of payment:

Order Form

Order no:

Order date:

Customer Details

Name: _____

Phone number: _____

Address: _____

_____

Delivery date: _____

Email: _____

Cake Details

Tiers: _____

Size & shapes: _____

Special instructions: _____

Cake :

Color scheme: _____

Flavours: _____

Notes

_____

_____

_____

_____

_____

Total cost:

Form of payment:

| Order no: | **Order Form** | Order date: |

Customer Details

Name:_____ Delivery date: _____

Phone number:_____ Email: _____

Address: _____

_____

_____

Cake Details

Tiers:_____ Color scheme:_____

Size & shapes:_____ Flavours:_____

Special instructions: _____

Cake :

Notes

_____

_____

_____

_____

_____

| Total cost: | Form of payment: |

Order Form

Order no:

Order date:

Customer Details

Name:

Phone number:

Address:

Delivery date:

Email:

Cake Details

Tiers:

Size & shapes:

Special instructions:

Cake :

Color scheme:

Flavours:

Notes

Total cost:

Form of payment:

| Order no: | **Order Form** | Order date: |

Customer Details

Name:_____ Delivery date:_____

Phone number:_____ Email:_____

Address:_____

_____

Cake Details

Tiers:_____ Color scheme:_____

Size & shapes:_____ Flavours:_____

Special instructions:_____

Cake :

Notes

_____

_____

_____

_____

_____

| Total cost: | Form of payment: |

Order Form

Order no:

Order date:

Customer Details

Name: _____

Phone number: _____

Address: _____

_____

Delivery date: _____

Email: _____

Cake Details

Tiers: _____

Size & shapes: _____

Special instructions: _____

Cake :

Color scheme: _____

Flavours: _____

Notes

_____

_____

_____

_____

_____

Total cost:

Form of payment:

Order Form

Order no:

Order date:

Customer Details

Name: _____

Phone number: _____

Address: _____

_____

Delivery date: _____

Email: _____

Cake Details

Tiers: _____

Size & shapes: _____

Special instructions: _____

Cake :

Color scheme: _____

Flavours: _____

Notes

_____

_____

_____

_____

Total cost:

Form of payment:

Order Form

Order no:

Order date:

Customer Details

Name:_____

Phone number:_____

Address:_____

_____

Delivery date: _____

Email: _____

Cake Details

Tiers:_____

Size & shapes:_____

Special instructions: _____

Cake : . . . .

Color scheme:_____

Flavours:_____

Notes

_____

_____

_____

_____

_____

Total cost:

Form of payment:

Order Form

Order no:

Order date:

Customer Details

Name: _____

Phone number: _____

Address: _____

_____

Delivery date: _____

Email: _____

Cake Details

Tiers: _____

Size & shapes: _____

Special instructions: _____

Color scheme: _____

Flavours: _____

Cake :

Notes

_____

_____

_____

_____

_____

Total cost:

Form of payment:

| Order no: | **Order Form** | Order date: |

Customer Details

Name:_____ Delivery date: _____

Phone number:_____ Email: _____

Address: _____

_____

Cake Details

Tiers:_____ Color scheme:_____

Size & shapes:_____ Flavours:_____

Special instructions: _____

Cake :

Notes

_____

_____

_____

_____

| Total cost: | Form of payment: |

Order no:	**Order Form**	Order date:

Customer Details

Name: _____ Delivery date: _____

Phone number: _____ Email: _____

Address: _____

_____

Cake Details

Tiers: _____ Color scheme: _____

Size & shapes: _____ Flavours: _____

Special instructions: _____

Cake :

Notes

_____

_____

_____

_____

_____

Total cost:	Form of payment:

Notes

Notes

Notes

Notes

Printed in Great Britain
by Amazon